METEOROLOGIST'S
TOOLS

ANDERS HANSON

Consulting Editor, Diane Craig, M.A./Reading Specialist

A Division of ABDO

ABDO
Publishing Company

visit us at www.abdopublishing.com

Published by ABDO Publishing Company, a division of ABDO,
P.O. Box 398166, Minneapolis, Minnesota 55439. Copyright © 2011
by Abdo Consulting Group, Inc. International copyrights reserved in
all countries. No part of this book may be reproduced in any form
without written permission from the publisher. Super SandCastle™
is a trademark and logo of ABDO Publishing Company.

Printed in the United States of America,
North Mankato, Minnesota
092010
012011

 PRINTED ON RECYCLED PAPER

Editor: Liz Salzmann
Content Developer: Nancy Tuminelly
Photo Credits: Anders Hanson, Shutterstock
With special thanks to Courtney, Denise, Gretchen, and Susie at
WeatherNation™ (www.weathernation.net)

Library of Congress Cataloging-in-Publication Data

Hanson, Anders, 1980-
 Meteorologist's tools / Anders Hanson.
    p. cm. -- (Professional tools)
 ISBN 978-1-61613-580-5
 1. Meteorological instruments--Juvenile literature. 2. Barome-
ters--Juvenile literature. 3. Thermometers--Juvenile literature. 4.
Meteorologists--Juvenile literature. I. Title.
 QC876.5.H36 2011
 551.5028'4--dc22
                        2010018609

Super SandCastle™ books are created by a team of professional
educators, reading specialists, and content developers around
five essential components—phonemic awareness, phonics,
vocabulary, text comprehension, and fluency—to assist young
readers as they develop reading skills and strategies and
increase their general knowledge. All books are written,
reviewed, and leveled for guided reading, early reading
intervention, and Accelerated Reader® programs for use in
shared, guided, and independent reading and writing activities to
support a balanced approach to literacy instruction.

CONTENTS

MEET A METEOROLOGIST

WHAT DOES A METEOROLOGIST DO?

Meteorologists study the **atmosphere**. Learning about the atmosphere helps them **predict** the weather.

WHY DO METEOROLOGISTS NEED TOOLS?

Tools help meteorologists do their jobs. They use tools to measure, record, and display **information** about the atmosphere.

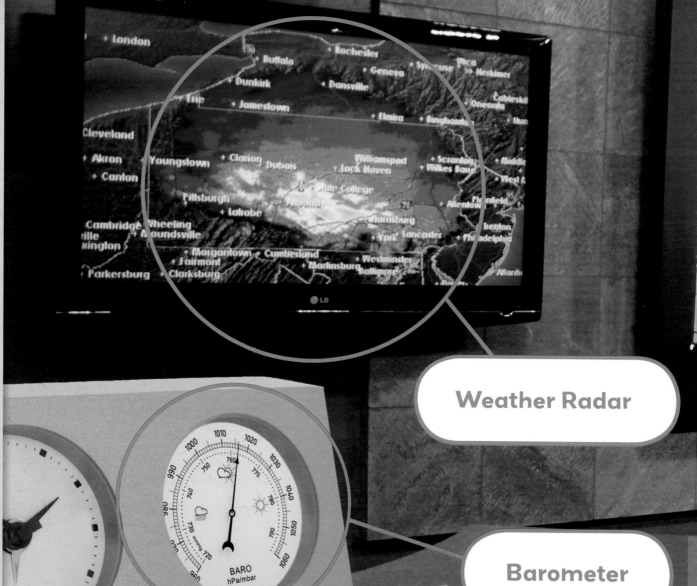

METEOROLOGIST'S TOOLS

Weather Radar

Barometer

Computer Model

Thermometer

BAROMETER

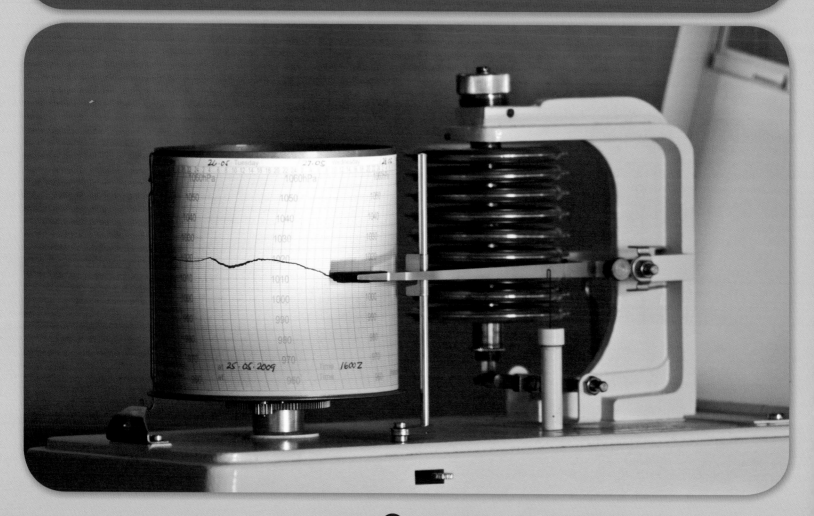

A barometer measures air pressure.

The earth is surrounded by air. Air has weight. Air pressure is the weight of the air on the earth.

When the air pressure is low, it is often cloudy. High pressure means it will probably be sunny. When the air pressure changes quickly, it usually gets windy.

Ethan is a meteorologist. He reads a barometer to see if the air pressure has changed.

Gretchen points to a high-pressure area on the map. It is probably sunny there.

WEATHER RADAR

Weather radar is used to find rain.

The radar station sends out a signal. When the signal hits water in the air, it bounces back. The longer it takes the signal to return, the farther away the rain is.

Weather radar can also show how hard it is raining. And it shows which way a storm is moving.

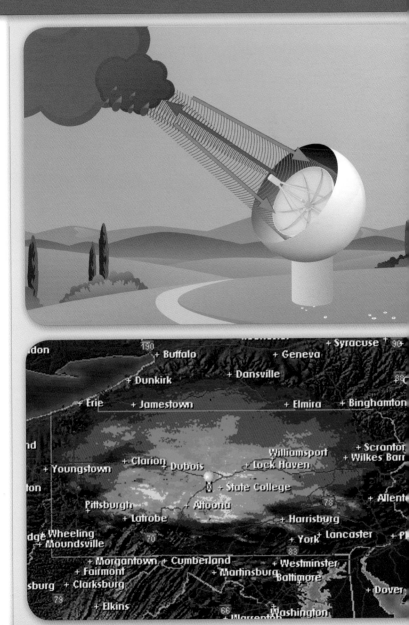

Information from the radar is shown on maps. Denise is pointing to a big storm.

Gretchen is in front of a green screen. On TV, the radar map shows instead of the green screen.

THERMOMETER

A thermometer measures the temperature.

A thermometer is often part of a weather station. Weather stations measure a lot of different things. They measure temperature, wind speed, and rain.

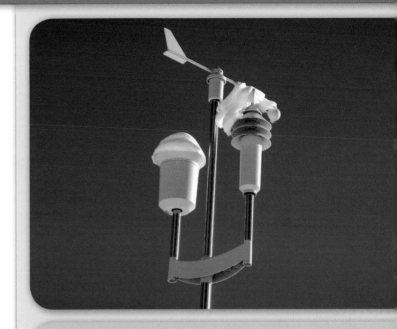

Susie checks the temperature on a thermometer.
It's in the shade, so it shows the correct temperature!

Gretchen looks at a weather station. It shows the inside and outside temperatures.

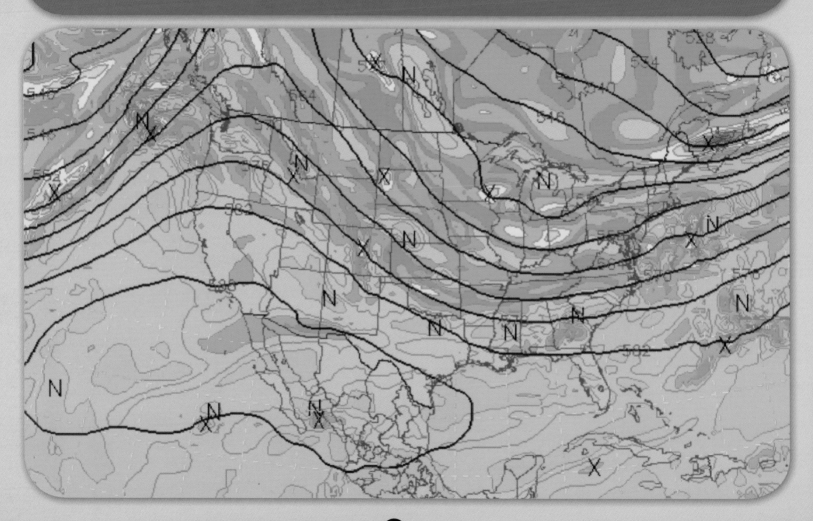

A computer model is used to forecast the weather.

Computer models use a lot of **information**. The information comes from barometers, radar stations, and thermometers.

Computer models use the information and math to **predict** the weather.

The **forecasts** are shown on colorful maps.

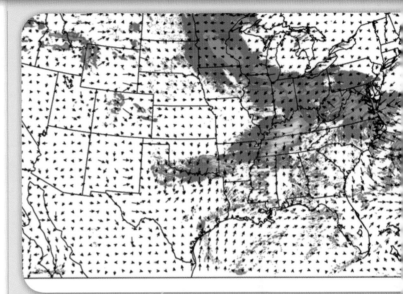

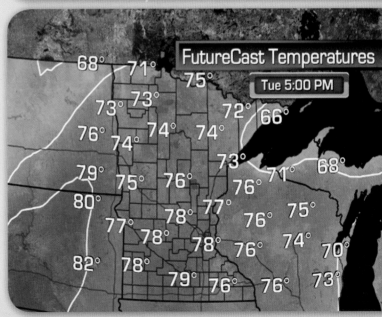

Gretchen looks at a computer model. The red and pink areas show where it will be really hot.

Denise is working with a computer model. It shows where it might rain.

MATCH THE WORDS TO THE PICTURES!

The answers are on the bottom of the page.

MATCH GAME

1. barometer

a.

2. weather radar

b.

3. thermometer

c.

4. computer model

d.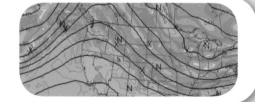

TEST YOUR TOOL KNOWLEDGE!

The answers are on the bottom of the page.

TOOL QUIZ

1.

A barometer measures temperature.

TRUE OR FALSE?

2.

A radar station sends out signals.

TRUE OR FALSE?

3.

A thermometer measures air pressure.

TRUE OR FALSE?

4.

A computer model uses math to figure out weather.

TRUE OR FALSE?

Answers: 1) false 2) true 3) false 4) true

atmosphere – the air that surrounds the earth.

degree – the unit used to measure temperature.

dial – a device on which a measurement is indicated by a moving pointer.

forecast – 1) a statement of what is likely to happen in the future based on facts and information.
2) to make a forecast.

graph – a chart or illustration that shows information about the amount of something.

hurricane – a tropical storm with very high winds that starts in the ocean and moves toward land.

information – the facts known about an event or subject.

isobar – a line on a weather map that shows where the air pressure is the same.

predict – to say what will happen in the future.